Rock Your Room

Laura Torres

QEB Publishing

Editor: Eve Marleau
Designer: Lisa Peacock
Photographer: Simon Pask
Project Maker: Dani Hall

Library of Congress Cataloging-in-Publication Data
Torres, Laura.
  Room / Laura Torres.
    p. cm. -- (QEB rock your ..)
  ISBN 978-1-59566-938-4 (library binding)
 1. Handicraft--Juvenile literature. 2. Interior decoration--Juvenile literature. 3. Bedrooms--Juvenile literature. I. Title.
  TT160.T5743 2011
  746--dc22

              2010010669

Printed in China

Copyright © QEB Publishing, Inc. 2010
Published in the United States by
QEB Publishing, Inc.
3 Wrigley, Suite A
Irvine, CA 92618

www.qed-publishing.co.uk

⚠ **WARNING**
On pages where you see this symbol, ask an adult for help.

Contents

Get the basics

Does your room need a makeover? There's no need to spend a lot of money redecorating. With a few materials and a little crafty instruction, you can turn your room into one-of-a-kind space that is all about YOU.

If you don't have exactly what you need for every project, you can often improvise and come up with something original. For example, if you don't have pebbles for the pebble picture frame, you can use shells or twigs instead.

Here are a few of the basic craft items you will need for some of the projects:

Glitter—Any kind of glitter works with the projects in the book, from fine to chunky. You can even use tiny beads or microbeads instead.

Flat-back rhinestones—These are inexpensive and come in small packages from a craft or jewelery-making store. You can substitute beads, glitter, or sequins if you can't get hold of rhinestones.

Glue—If a project calls for "glue" you can use whatever you might have around the house. "White glue" means a white standard glue. "Craft glue" means a thick white glue that won't run or spread.

Scissors—Make sure you always have a good pair of scissors for cutting things such as paper, felt, and yarn in the projects.

Always remember...
When making a project, protect the surface you are working on with newspaper or plastic for a mess-free, easy clean-up.

The perfect pebble frame

You and your friends will be picture perfect in this pebble frame. You can find these glass pebbles in most florists.

Step 1

Spread a thick layer of glue on a small section of the frame with the toothpick or stick.

Step 2

Stick the pebbles in the glue, working quickly so it doesn't dry. Sprinkle glitter in between the pebbles.

Step 3

Repeat the steps until you have covered the front of the frame in pebbles and glitter.

Step 4

When the frame is completely dry, tap off the extra glitter.

For a cool, rock star look, use darker pebbles and silver glitter.

Starry night box

Make a special keepsake box for all your treasures. This cosmic design will rock any bedroom.

YOU WILL NEED

- Shoebox
- Dark blue or purple acrylic paint
- Paintbrush
- Five large wooden beads
- Glue
- Opaque gel pens or metallic permanent markers

Why not paint your box with brightly colored springtime flowers instead?

Step 1

Glue one bead on each corner of the bottom of the box to make feet.

Step 2

Glue another bead on top of the lid in the center to form a handle.

Step 3

Let the glue dry. Paint the box and the beads with the acrylic paint.

Step 4

Once the paint is dry, use the gel pens or metallic markers to draw starry shapes and cosmic planets on the box.

Crazy Coil photo string

Here's a unique way to display pictures of your friends and decorate your room at the same time.

Step 1

Cut the straws into several 1 inch (2. 5 centimeter) sections. Cut the craft foam into small squares and diamonds.

Step 2

Thread pieces of the straw onto the fishing line, then push the needle through the craft foam to thread the line.

Step 3

Repeat step 2 several times, until the line is almost full. Tie the end of the line around a piece of straw to secure it.

Step 4

Twist a pipe cleaner between two straws. Coil both ends of the pipe cleaner. Repeat several times, spacing them evenly.

Customized cork

Why settle for plain old cork? It's easy to decorate your cork board to match your room. All you need is some acrylic paint and a pom-pom trim.

YOU WILL NEED

- Plain cork board
- Masking tape
- Acrylic paints
- Paintbrush
- Heavy-duty craft glue
- Pom-pom trim

Step 1

If your cork board has a frame, put masking tape around the edges to protect the frame from the paint.

Step 2

Paint the front of the cork board with acrylic paint. Let dry. Give the cork board a second coat of paint. Let dry.

Step 3

Paint designs on the cork board. Remove the masking tape from the frame.

Step 4

Glue the pom-pom trim to the frame with craft glue, then let dry.

Paint your cork board with a camouflage pattern for a cool, military style.

CD suncatcher

YOU WILL NEED
• Two old or blank CDs
• Fabric paint
• Flatback rhinestones
• Piece of colored yarn or string, about 1 foot (33 centimeters) long
• Glue
• Scissors
• Decorative bead (optional)

Hang this CD sparkler next to a window. It will catch the sunlight and turn your room into a rainbow of colors.

Create a cosmic design with blue fabric paints and bright stars instead of rhinestones.

Step 1

Paint a design on to the shiny side of the CD with the fabric paint.

Step 2

Before it dries, stick the rhinestones into the paint. Let the fabric paint dry completely. The dry paint will hold the rhinestones in place.

Step 3

Spread glue on the opposite side of one of the CDs.

Step 4

Put the yarn across the middle of one of the CDs so a small part is hanging over one end, and the rest over the other. Stick the CDs together.

Step 5

When the glue is dry, trim off the shorter side of the yarn or string or tie a bead on to it. Hang your suncatcher in a sunny place.

T-shirt art attack

If you have a favorite T-shirt that you've grown out of, don't throw it out—turn it into a work of art!

Step 1

Place the styrofoam on top of the T-shirt. Cut around it, leaving about 2.5 inches (5 centimeters) extra on each side.

◄ Cut out a cool cartoon or an old sports shirt to hang on your bedroom wall.

Step 2

Fold the excess fabric around the styrofoam, making neat folds at the corners.

Step 3

Use the double-sided tape to secure the T-shirt firmly around the styrofoam.

Step 4

Cut a 12 inch (30 centimeter) length of yarn. Tape the yarn 2.5 inches (5 centimeters) down from the top of the T-shirt.

Step 5

Cut a piece of card to cover the back of the T-shirt, then use the double-sided tape to fix in place.

Dragonfly flutter clips

Turn plain clothespins into shimmering, shiny dragonflies. You can clip them to lampshades, drapes, and books around your room.

➡ Use pink netting and satin for the wings to make a floaty, fairy-like dragonfly.

Step 1

Clip the clothespin to the edge of the paper cup. Put some rocks or a heavy object in the cup to stop it falling over.

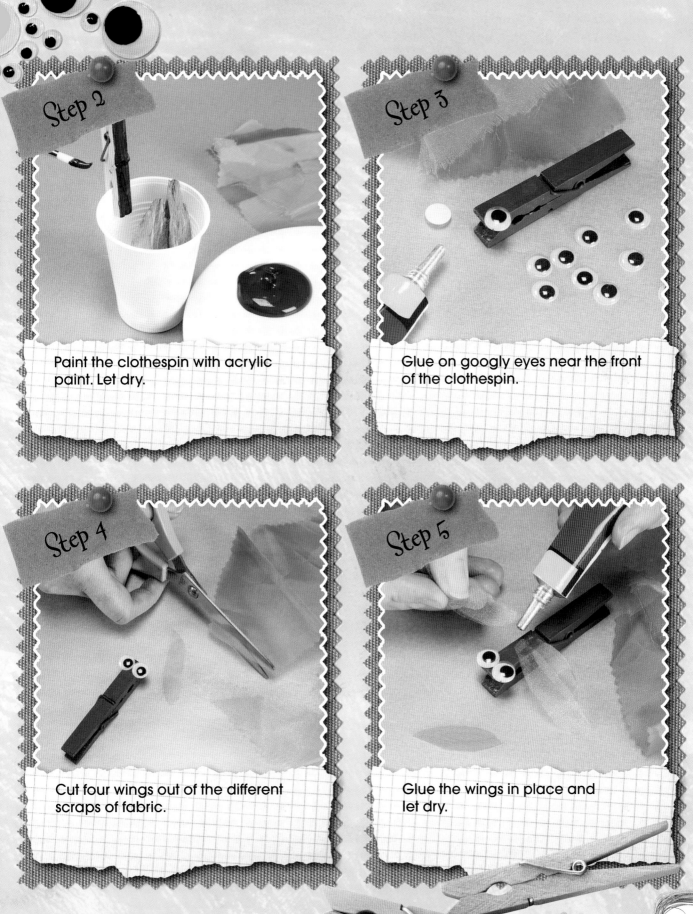

Step 2

Paint the clothespin with acrylic paint. Let dry.

Step 3

Glue on googly eyes near the front of the clothespin.

Step 4

Cut four wings out of the different scraps of fabric.

Step 5

Glue the wings in place and let dry.

Matchbox mini-dresser

A small chest of drawers can hold coins, notes, earrings, and other small treasures. Use some matchboxes to make a mini-treasure chest!

Step 1

Use the glue to stick the matchboxes together in a stack. Let dry.

Step 2

Cut a piece of paper to wrap around the outside of the dresser. Fold around the boxes and trim to fit.

Step 3

Glue the paper in place, with the seam at the bottom of the chest.

Use dark-blue and ➡ sparkling silver paper to make a space-age keepsake box.

Step 4

Trace the ends of the matchbox drawers on the paper. Cut out the paper and glue each piece on the front of each drawer.

Step 5

Lay the chest on its back and glue a bead in the middle of each drawer. Let dry.

Scary monster tacks

Liven up a bulletin board with these fuzzy, googly-eyed tacks. You can make them in several different colors to create a scary world of monsters!

Step 1

Using the craft glue, stick the top end of a tack onto a fuzzy pom-pom.

Step 2

Cut a small piece of red felt, about 0.2 inches (0.5 centimeters) long, to make a tongue.

Stick two eyes on the pom-pom on the opposite side to the tack.

Draw a small black line in the middle of the tongue, then glue it just below the googly eyes.

Make a flower tack using a foam pad and some glitter.

23

Big, bold bedroom banner

YOU WILL NEED
- Drinking straw
- Yarn or string
- Different-colored felt
- Scissors
- Craft glue

You can hang this colorful, personalized flag on your bedroom door or on your wall.

Cut flower shapes out of felt to make a colorful summer garden banner.

Step 1

Cut a piece of yarn about 3 foot (1 meter) long. Thread the yarn through the straw and tie the ends together.

Step 2

Cut a felt flag almost as wide as the straw, and about 2 inches (5 centimeters) longer than you want it to be when it's finished.

Step 3

Wrap the top of the flag over the straw and glue it in place.

Step 4

Cut felt shapes to go on your flag and glue them in place. Let the glue dry, then hang the flag up.

Bright night candle holder

You can turn any glass jar into a stained glass masterpiece. All you need is glue and paint!

Cover your jar with hearts and butterflies to give it a bright, summery feel.

Step 1

Use the black fabric paint to draw a design on the jar or bottle. Let dry.

Step 2

Put 1 tablespoon of glue and a few drops of acrylic paint in the paper cups for each color. Mix with the spoons or craft sticks.

Step 3

Use the paintbrush to fill in the outlined shapes with the glue paint.

Step 4

Let the glue paint dry. Ask an adult to help you put a candle in the jar, or put it on a windowsill.

Mega-monster pencil holder

Made from recycled materials, this pencil holder is cute and practical. A great way to store all your stationery!

Make some teeth with white felt to create a scary stationery monster!

Step 1

Cut a piece of felt the right size to wrap around your can. Trim the edges to fit, if necessary.

28

Step 2

Using the craft glue, stick one end of the felt on the can. Put some glue on the felt, then wrap it around the can.

Step 3

Make eyes with the black and white felt, then make ears and a nose with the colored felt.

Step 4

Glue the ears, eyes, and nose pieces onto the can.

Step 5

Cut six pieces of yarn, around 1.2 inches (3 centimeters) long. Glue them onto the can to make whiskers.

Rock a recycled style

If you don't have everything you need for the projects in this book you can customize each item with what you have around the house. Your projects won't just be unique—if you use recycled items it'll be better for the environment, too. Being green rocks!

Page 6

The perfect pebble frame

Instead of buying glass pebbles, try using small rocks, shells, or large beads you may already have around the house.

Page 12

Customized cork

Recycled cork coasters make cool mini-bulletin boards. Hang them in a group for a big impact.

Page 18

Dragonfly flutter clips

If you don't have any fabric scraps, you can make wings out of a plastic shopping bag, a net fruit bag, or even tracing paper.

Matchbox mini-dresser

Try using recycled gift wrap or a colorful page from a magazine to decorate your dresser.

Scary monster tacks

Don't throw away games or puzzles if you are missing some of the pieces. Glue leftover pieces on tacks instead of fuzzy pom-poms.

Bright night candle holder

Use a recycled bottle or jar for this project. If the jar or bottle has a label on it, soak it for half an hour in warm water. It should peel off easily. Remove any glue residue and dry thoroughly before you paint on it.

Pencil holder

A plastic juice carton works well for this project. You can also use a large plastic yoghurt tub. Make sure you wash and dry out your container before you start the project.

Index